Anesthesia

Anesthesia

poems

KENNY FRIES

The Advocado Press

Published by
The Advocado Press, P.O. Box 145, Louisville, KY 40201

First Edition

Cover design by Michael Ian Kaye
Cover Art "Scissors and Bone" by Carlyle Poteat
Book Design by Eve L. Kirch
Production by Maria Burtis

Library of Congress Catalog Card Number: 96-85839

ISBN: 0-9627064-6-9

For my parents
and in memory of
Joseph Milgram, M.D.
(1900–1989)

CONTENTS

*Remember that under the skin you fondle lie the bones,
waiting to reveal themselves.*

— IKKYU

I
ANESTHESIA

Anesthesia

the night surrounds
skin and the moon   full
sends yellow light through

on cold nights
silence magnifies sound
and an elevator closing

to a child is an end
an amputation
you see   they have taken

my memory   the memory
of my own body   soundless   senseless
tearing of the skin

once belonging
to a three-month baby boy

there are scars in a cold night sky
touch them
touch them and imagine

a child buried
in silence   footsteps
make him reach

beneath white sheets   feet
once a child's
feet still kicking

I want to hold them
as if they were
my lover

but pain
like time happens even
while you sleep

Excavation

1. Excavation

Tonight, when I take off my shoes:
three toes on each twisted foot.

I touch the rough skin. The holes
where the pins were. The scars.

If I touch them long enough will I find
those who never touched me? Or those

who did? *Freak, midget, three-toed
bastard.* Words I've always heard.

Disabled, crippled, deformed. Words
I was given. But tonight I go back

farther, want more, tear deeper into
my skin. Peeling it back I reveal

the bones at birth I wasn't given—
the place where no one speaks a word.

2. Incubator

As if from a goldfish bowl, through
small, fogged eyes. And nowhere

do I find you, even though I know
you must have been there. The hands

that turn me are the nurse's hands;
the eyes watching are my father's.

But where is the body from which I was
born unwhole? Your body almost

died giving birth to mine. Mother,
after all these years I am asking why

you never told me. We touch through
a sheet of glass. Give me your hand—

help me find those missing bones, clear
that infant's eyes. Open them—wider.

3. X-Ray

I am eight months old and looking
for you, daddy, at the other

end of the metal table. Your eyes
told me all I need to know—

if I could just remember. I watch
the large machine rattle down its track,

feel the cold on my skin,
when all these years I wanted

the memory of your hands holding my
twisted feet in the right position.

Remembering this now I am
still that eight month old,

your son, staring into the eyes
of that machine, trying to find you

in the reflection it gives back
—nothing from the waist down.

4. Learning to Walk

There is light at the end of the narrow hall.
Enclosed in a cast, my shorter leg reaches

for the ground. My knee can't bend. Scrapes
against the plaster wall. My toes above

the carpet. If I press them to the ground,
the cast will break, my leg will crack—

If I close my eyes? If I don't look down?
The hall, narrow as the cast, held by pins,

my leg inside. No bone will hold my weight.
No arms will end my fall. Palms pressed against

the dark canal, I lift my weight. How far
is the light? With open eyes—my foot on ground.

5. Body Language

What is a scar if not the memory of a once open wound?
You press your finger between my toes, slide

the soap up the side of my leg, until you reach
the scar with the two holes, where the pins were

inserted twenty years ago. Leaning back, I
remember how I pulled the pin from my leg, how

in a waist-high cast, I dragged myself
from my room to show my parents what I had done.

Your hand on my scar brings me back to the tub
and I want to ask you: What do you feel

when you touch me there? I want you to ask me:
What are you feeling now? But we do not speak.

You drop the soap in the water and I continue
washing, alone. Do you know my father would

bathe my feet, as you do, as if it was the most
natural thing. But up to now, I have allowed

only two pair of hands to touch me there,
to be the salve for what still feels like an open wound.

The skin has healed but the scars grow deeper—
When you touch them what do they tell you about my life?

Brotherly Love

In the room with the orange carpet,
every night your hands

under my blanket. I remember how
you touched me. *What did you want?*

What did I give you?
I still know that room

where everything was yours.
I feel your hands around my neck,

the carpet burns
on my thigh. You'd never let me sleep.

*Is there no way to rid you
from my dreams?*

I wake hitting the lover
sleeping at my side.

Love Poem

On the narrow bed. Patterns of light
and shadow across your body. I hold

your face in my hands. Tell me, before
I kiss you, what is it like to be

so beautiful? I want to know how other
hands have touched you. What other

eyes, beneath your clothes, imagine.
And how do you imagine me? Do you

feel my callused skin? See my twisted
bones? When you take off my clothes

will you kiss me all over? Touch me as
if my body were yours. Make me beautiful.

Transfiguration

All night, I explore the contours
of your legs. Fitting my hands

around your knees, I know—*solid*—.
I knead the muscles of your calves,

hold your ankles, tightly. Your skin
surprises my lips and I want to drink

your smoothness. How else can I quench
this thirst? I want to break your bones.

Make them mine. Your body holds all
the secrets. Give them to me now—

in the dark. Your smooth skin over
my twisted bones—the perfect disguise.

Dressing The Wound

When you take off my clothes, the fire
heats my skin. I surround your nipples

with my toes. In front of me, your lips
find my scars, peel back my broken skin.

Why do I let your kiss expose my bones?
Trembling, I hear them crack.

When I open my eyes: my feet, twisted,
in your palms. Molded by your fingers,

my six toes. But . . . *gentle*. When you hold
my legs, it is my heart your hands enfold.

History

Begin with innocence. Then, the missing
bones. When did it happen? Who knows

how loss occurs? No photographs. No
memory. This is what I have

to go on: the hospital report,
my father's words. In front of me:

my feet, each the size of his finger.
Now, the gnarled roots of trees.

For thirty years, this question: how
do you mourn for something you never had?

Remains

Each night, you carved your name into my skin.
I gave myself to you, willingly.

Your body, abundant to my hands. My body,
insignificant. . . .

But tonight, I open my eyes: our bodies—
face to face, chest to chest, groin to groin.

Your arms embrace me and I am whole. We are
of measure. I whisper: *never let me go*. . . .

You always do. What remains is the taste
of blood. On my skin, the stain.

Surgery

these nights I miss your hands
your mouth chewing on my nipples
your fingers

into me   the slight scrape
of uncut nails

you leave no scars

years from now
how will I know
you have been here with me

II
SATURN RETURN

Elegy

We lose them, one
by one, like years,
or days, or
hours.

When at night I
turn the lights out
building a darkness
they appear again—

as voices,
or a burst
of solitary laughter.

And that day, at the
rock where they threw
your ashes—you were there,
walking toward me

on the path at the edge
of the hill below, waving
back to me, smiling.

Returns

A landscape hardly exists at all,
because its appearance is constantly
changing; it lives by virtue of its
surroundings . . . which vary continually.
— CLAUDE MONET

1.

To go back. Once. Then,
again: grainstacks, cliffs,
the cathedral—at

different times, in
other light, another
season. What is he looking

for? What draws him
to stand
in the same place—

is the object changed
by the elements outside it?
That light is gone. And,

the moment: a series
of movements, within
a larger movement. It is

this he longs to
capture. What else
if not to pass our eyes

over the same skin. How
many times? Your eyes,
so innocent the day we met

turn dangerous at night. Your
lips caress the wine, later
my tongue. Your hands

the grainstacks, your
thighs the cliffs, your face
the cathedral. What are these

words if not the returns—
to a lover's side or to
a memory. . . . Still, we forget

not the object
but viewing it we also see
the passing of our lives.

2.

To render you is an act
of imprecision; not a lie.
Like the painter who stands

in the same place but shifts
the scene, slightly, on each
canvas—for effect? A balanced

composition? More grass, the
poplar with different branches,
the stacks more distant from

each other. Does the sun
cause the stone to be that
color? *Don't cut down the trees,*

he said, *I am not yet
finished*. He plucked the leaves
off the oak so he could still

paint it as winter. Later,
in his studio he renders it
from memory—as I render

you: Is your skin that
smooth? Your thighs
that strong? Your chest

formed by such a delicate line?
I use a simple palette.
A single stroke to capture

the intricate surface
of desire. Words
on a page, the artist's eye—

turn what we love into
those clouds
conveniently arranged in the sky.

3.

To choose the object of
return, the body to compel
desire. What drives him to

persist? The poplars
sway, the cathedral
stands, a grainstack

next to houses. From this he
sees how people live—the symbols
of his nation. Older,

he paints the Seine, its
morning light the past,
its movement more than

nature. *I return to you
because you opened me.* Your
hairless skin, your sharp

blue eyes, the broadness of
your shoulders. Why does your body
wind its way back into

mine? Like those slender
trunks, that sculpted
stone, the cliffs

where land meets sea.
From earth and skin,
from sky and bone, we choose

our field of vision.
A different view, a later
hour, *one more time*—

and stone can live:
a cathedral
flesh and flower.

How It Was

New Year's Eve—
no, after
midnight, so

New Year's Day. But
always the pressure
as you find your way

inside me. I am
lifted, my back
arched, almost

breaking—balanced
on the edge
of your finger—Oh,

how the sounds
escape from me, come
with laughter—

how you want me
as you push
into—gently,

deeper—that awful
lovely place
I desire.

Saturn Return

you sat with us in the Italian restaurant
the year before you did not wear your shawl
wrapped around your shoulders it

enveloped us like your story of the healer
in the tent north of San Francisco
you did not stay, you said, even if

he could heal you—his politics
were wrong, believing only men, nothing
feminine could rule our country

Kathy, it is my birthday again
one year later the restaurant has burned
and I am in Virginia remembering

what you told us: no longer attached to living
a long life, the weakness of your flesh releasing
your spirit   I could not believe

the last time I saw your face it was
the mask of a crone, and after
a lunch you barely ate you retired

to your room, where you sat in bed throwing
kisses—

but I still hear your voice, and in your picture
your finger points—
and I swear I see it moving

Getting To Yes

I remove your clothes
slowly,
your t-shirt
over your arms,

begin to knead your
muscles, down
your lower back,
and discover

the delicate
dark hair
surrounding
your spine.

I hold your thighs.
Slip my palm
under your shorts,
loosen them

as I open your mouth
with my tongue
and your teeth
capture

my tongue and
my fingers find
the most
vulnerable place—

where I know
if I enter
it will end
your silence.

Jerusalem: 1984

1

they leave poisoned scraps of food
to kill cats that stray into the Jewish Quarter
of the Old City in Jerusalem

and in the Moslem Quarter Arab women balance
baskets on their heads
as they walk through the market where

lambs are tied in front
of stalls selling food
to tourists who ride

camels out of Jaffa Gate
where fellow pilgrims wait to clap
and click their cameras

I arrive on *Yom Yerusahalayim*   the day
celebrating the reunification
of the Holy City

at two a.m. a large black car drove
up to the Western Wall and led
by dancing yeshiva boys the Chief Rabbi

led the joyous throng in prayer before driving
off into the city
beyond the walls

2

> *(for Peter*

in your Arab village I spent the night
with you, an American, friend
of a friend

the calls of Ramadan rode
from the tower on the hot night air
into your room

we could walk arm in arm through your village, you said
but if I was a woman I could not
spend this night with you

in such a different freedom two Jewish men
embracing under foreign sounds
in an ancient home

3

(for Micha

part of your home dates back
to Crusader times and I wonder how old
the graves are when you show me where

men can meet men in Independence Park
in Jerusalem you are safe
protected by soldiers' guns you live

so close to the Wall, I say
this is your sign from God
you belong among your people
Dutch   gay   Jew

I want to think when crowds rush home
on Friday afternoons in San Francisco
they are rushing for the same reason

people rush home here
to welcome the Sabbath angel

What Venice Remembers

*. . . and nothing shall purge your
deaths from our memories.
For our memories are your only
graves.*

— ANDRE TONC

today the synagogues are closed for prayer
the museum is not open   I have forgotten
a holy day   Shavuoth   when God gave his word

but Venice you, too, gave us a word   *ghetto*
and on this day I remember that once
an iron foundry existed here

until you took your Jews
surrounded them by walls
closed in at night by an iron gate

all that remains of these gates
are the signs which were placed at their side
and two walled-up windows where the guards watched

this is the northern corner of Venice
where the houses reach higher for the sky
where the streets narrow then open

on a square there hangs a neon Jewish star
above a religious shop
here Jewish tourists congregate, arriving

from all directions they stand
and stare at a monument remembering *the masses
for the gas chambers, the masses advancing*

under the whip of the executioner
the precise dates are given
December 5, 1943   August 17, 1944

what was started here in 1516
continued on December 5, 1943
and who among you raised a hand

who in this city of water
shed a tear   August 17 was many months away
there is no monument to what happened here

this is the poorest quarter now
no flowers line the streets
but the houses still remember

they reach up like outstretched arms lifted to the sky
and at any moment might suddenly collapse
downward to the ground

The Burden of Memory

they tell us   remember
six million Jews   killed
and I remember

my father told me   remember
and I tried
to tell him

the pink triangle
lower than
the yellow star

and I tried to tell him
my legs are not
perfect   I would have been

undesirable
they tell us   remember
six million Jews   murdered

and I remember
in *The Village Voice*
an historian in California knows

six million Jews   alive
hiding beneath
the New York City subway

they tell us   remember
six million Jews   exterminated
and in movies   trains

symbols of walking
to death
and they cannot

imagine a happy ending

they tell us   remember
and I remember
outside *Ya'ad Vashem*

the Holocaust museum
in Jerusalem
there is a boat

Denmark sailed seven thousand Jews

to safety
and a garden
planted by survivors

to remember
those who saved them
(*Ya'ad Vashem*   a hand and a name)

and I remember my father
praying to this God
but I cannot believe

an imperfect God
who lets his chosen people
die   an imperfect God

who made my legs imperfect
I remember
Hasidic Jews in Borough Park

listening to the radio
and waiting for the Messiah
FDR did not

bomb Auschwitz but
the Americans did liberate
the concentration camps

my father told me   remember
six millions Jews   killed
but not of a distant cousin

hid
on a farm in Southern France
Christians saved him

and though we can find
our saviors
we still remember

the stars, the trains,
hear the lies
yes

I remember
six million Jews   killed
and others saved

they tell us
this could not happen
here   I remember

bombs not dropped
words not spoken
action not taken

and ask   who
will save us

and who will save
my Jewish lover

and know
saving was not enough
and if saving is not enough

what is

tell me the answer
I will remember

In These Times

*crisis: the turning point in the course of a
disease when it becomes clear whether
the patient will live or die.*
　　　　　　　—WEBSTER'S DEFINITION

Do little things. Every day.
　　　　　　　— ST. THERESE

1

in the morning　 the sun
angles through the window
spreads light and shadow

on our bed　 I press
my lips against your back
start another one way conversation

I want to imitate the birds
travel great distances
only to return once

again to the same place
to sing about my flight
but today we are

together　 you are
safely protected in your sleep
I get dressed, I read the paper

I kiss your cheek and walk
downstairs to my car
drive down the hill

and begin the day

2

sometimes the laundry is enough

or to wake and smell
fresh brewed morning coffee

the simple walk to the corner store
or washing yesterday's dishes

I want to notice how the setting
sun changes the color of the hardwood floors

to watch the fog
move through our garden

to listen to our house
creak in the wind

3

I have slept in this bed
many times   but tonight
I cannot sleep

too many times I sit
at this desk asking   who
will die

I have been beneath the earth
where the water incessantly gorges

on rock   I have been where the land meets the sea
where cliffs bend back from the spray

I have found you by this rock
on this land   I have opened my arms to the water
to the sky and still I ask my question
what is this bed

what are these arms
what is the land and the sea

4

it has been too long since we touched

too long since I slid the callused side
of my mangled foot against the smoothness of your calf

Now
after your absence
and the days getting longer

Now
after two years of living together
surrounded by death   here
as everywhere

Now
I cannot wait
to kiss you again

we cannot wait
not one   more   minute

To The End

then we took it slow,
our last walk, re-

visiting the old lady who sells
peeled fruit in a plastic bag

her young grandchildren help
carry fruit to the cart

how you loved the limón, which looked
like orange, how I licked the spice
that looked like cinnamon off my fingers

we roamed the pier, checked
the ferry times; up the sand
streets where crazy dogs were barking

and back through town, past
the restaurant with the green parrot, where
we first saw Solomon the waif, past where
his drunken mother waited for his money, to our
hotel room with the fish tiles on the floor

we sat on the terrace, almost level with
the sea soaring through rocks—
I want to catch its water

in the large shells I watched you gather;
I want to splash
my feet in the shells' water as you hold them—

remember the clear still waters of the Contoy beach
remember the boat ride back to Puerto Juarez: the sun

burning on our faces
I still hear the music of our final drive

—of welcome, you said,
not departure

Solstice

Darkness comes early. The trees are almost
bare. As I lose the light, a thick fog

gathers at my door. Foghorns from the harbor.
Then, once again, I conjure you:

your limbs are fallen trees; cracked leaves
your hair. The fire breathes your breath

in every room, you're there. One morning
I will banish you, your body—forsworn.

No longer will I need those nights trembling
in your arms. I hold on to a tenuous dawn.

III
THE HEALING
NOTEBOOKS

for Alex

(1)

Our landlady brings us tomatoes, white
zucchini, cucumbers from her garden. Leaves

a bag of apples on our kitchen table. *Keep
you boys healthy*, she tells us after driving

fifty miles to take care of things when
they need fixing. Burton, the large man

she lives with, wants to fix the light
in your room. *Try it with a girl*, he says.

You smile in the hallway. *Mrs. Jordan,
will you paint the kitchen white? We need*

it brighter, you tell her. *Those girls
upstairs*, she says, *I have to paint them*

*first. In their bathroom the roof's been leaking.
Surprised it hasn't leaked down here yet.*

(2)

Late at night. Together in the tub
I face the faucet. I gently curve

my hands around your shoulders. *How long
has it been since we've been naked like this?*

I reach down your back to your thighs
as you move against me.

Did your teeth break skin? Look
at my neck. *Did you draw blood?*

(3)

You drag my arm across your body. You are wet.
I press my lips against the moisture.

I hear the electricity in the walls.
The red light from the tower—

What are you trying to tell me?
We slept with hammers by our bed.

Animal noises escaping from the closet.
Our television a house for spirits.

Now, we sleep, too comfortable, too long—
Wake up.

What is inside you never sleeps, wants
the edge, is dangerous.

Watch the moment.
It is nothing complacent.

(4)

The heat makes everything rise:
crickets in the brush, the deer

escaping across the meadow, an old
dog trying to find shade.

A starless night. I sleep sheetless
and dream of friends I haven't seen

for twenty years. The moon is Paul
and Kathy dead: I am naked.

I have been too long in these fields
climbing the hills, searching for the highest place

to see the mountains. I have answered
the calls of early morning birds, followed

tadpoles in the pond, watched
the rose bush blossom. I have held

ripened berries in my hand. Tasted them.
All this, and the blowing wind.

(5)

In bed next to you, I feel your heartbeat.
I follow your veins: the blood flowing

to each end of your body. I want to pour
all your blood from your body, to spill it

out of you, cleanse this invisible thing
from our lives. I want to wrap you in a blanket,

run with you far to the mountains, to the edge
of the sea. I want to find protection.

But the world is as it is. Blood is no longer
life. Positive, a different meaning now.

(6)

The wind knocks gently at the window.
Rain changes into snow. Swirling,

it brings you back to me—in your parents'
den, on the narrow bed, you are

lowering yourself onto me,
your sister on the way down

to meet me. Our first time.
We don't love like that any more.

Passion, that rusty hinge. Oh,
how I long to open that door

one more time, see your face
that way—wide and staring into me.

(7)

Why do I remember this now? Here,
passion invades like the winds

gusting through the valley.
The distant mountains mold your body

into flesh again. The dog finds deer
bones on the prairie, drops them at my door.

The four-sided sky mirrors my desire:
at dusk, all is silent. Herons fly

overhead; geese gather at the river.
Night brings dreams of you dying again

and a fresh blanket of snow.
It is spring. It will melt at dawn.

(8)

Mrs. Jordan insists the money
gets you sick in Mexico. *There's*

dirt on those pesos, she says, *you
put them in your mouth, that's where*

it comes from. My doctor says I got
shigala from the chicken, had the runs

on the customs line, lost ten pounds
in the hospital. But you're O.K.

even though you drank the water.
I was careful. We both touched

the money. But Mrs. Jordan knows.
She has relatives who live there.

(9)

During the night you disappear
beneath the blankets. I feel you

wet between my legs. I hold
your head in both my hands.

You come up for air. I smell
myself when you kiss me.

Do you remember the first time
undressing in your parents' house?

Do you remember calling me from the bar
telling me you had to see me again?

Do you remember how scared we were?

(10)

What has changed? It's not easy
to answer. *Razor blades?*

We no longer share.
My toothbrush? Thrown away

because he accidentally used it.
Deep kisses? Occasionally, but

not without wondering. . . . Shouldn't
we sip from different straws?

Small things. I'm always thinking
will this be the last healthy day?

*You'll drive yourself crazy
thinking that way.*

What has changed?
Our lives.

(11)

Not the way they hold me,
but the way they hold

the cup, the way your cheeks
rest on your knuckles, fingers

folded in, wrists out,
elbows on the table as

you read the newspaper
as we eat dinner, here

in this house, toward
the middle of our lives:

of all hands
your hands

of all men
you.

(12)

Begin with scraps of paper, odd
sentences, someone else's phrases—

*There is always something to be made
of pain.* But art is once removed,

the widow knitting scarves,
the lover quilting names,

where was I in 1981? '82? '83? *Ask
whose signature was stamped on the orders?*

Sarah says, *People with AIDS need drugs
not fiction about AIDS.* There, I use

the name in someone else's name.
Not one of my poems ever saved

one Jew. And still I sit all day as if
choosing the right word could save your life.

(13)

Voices across the lake—not yours
but unfamiliar laughter. This afternoon,

sitting on the dock, I watched the swallows
skim the surface of the lake. Without warning,

a large heron flew right before my eyes
and disappeared beyond the next cove.

I turned for your reaction—
you weren't there. I went inside.

All summer I've been talking to you
and you're not here. You told me

you didn't want to know I was afraid.
You said all I could write about was

your dying. Can't you see that's not
true. I'm writing about our lives.

(14)

In bed together watching the t.v. news,
flipping through the entertainment section

I notice Leontyne Price will be singing
somewhere outside the city. *We better go,*

you tell me, *might be the last time we get
to see her.* Are you saying this will be

her last appearance here? Or we may not
see her again together?

Or you at all. I don't ask
but think: What is love without

plans? Without a future? How will those
high notes sound without you?

(15)

Who knows the precise moment when the stream
will overflow? You look for signs: white

on your tongue, a red blotch growing
on your thigh, fungus between your toes.

Who knows when it begins? The rituals
of the worried well. The fear of the common

cold. Wouldn't it be easier if it happened
now? The inevitable wasting away,

the delirium. But who is immune to hope?
On a night like this who would keep

the window closed? Open it and hear
the stream flowing all night long.

(16)

Eileen calls to tell me the truth
about the trees: they are not dying

but storing sap, preparing for winter.
Eileen, it is not the trees, but

these leaves—the last gasp
of color last night windswept

off the trees. It is the leaf I am
holding, the orange burning

the heat of summer into my hand.
How else can I remember this orange

in the winter gray? How else can I
stop this leaf turning in my hand?

(17)

For days the clouds hide the mountain.
All week, through the haze, I track

our love. Why this longing now?
Not the longing of desire, not

sex, that was never the thing.
The longing for a safer time.

Last night, finally, the sun
pink behind the hills,

from the road you could see the sky,
for a moment it was there—

It's like the weather, I tell you.
Unstoppable, but of measure,

innocent as the questions
one following another: why

our love begins, and
as easy, is taken away.

(18)

Late afternoon. The sun
heats the room; clouds

shadow the hills. All day
I have tried to get back

to the beginning, to your question
at the bar while I sat on that stool.

Who knew one month later you would
bring secrets to my bed? Who knew

your blood was infected? Who wanted
to know? What was a t-cell in '84?

Now, we count them. Every three months
like our anniversaries that first year.

Do you know I blame myself for finding you?
Do you know I ask myself: did you find me

because you knew this
would happen? I find these

questions in the late afternoon:
What if we did know? What then?

(19)

From the west you approach me. To get here
you travel the same roads I travelled.

Was it light enough to see the valley
on your first descent from the mountains?

Did you reach the strangeness of the
Great Salt Basin in the afternoon?

Did you marvel at the sky blue of the Great
Salt Lake before you entered the city?

Closer, did you think of me? Did you think
the same thoughts as when you first approached

me, years ago, in the bar in New York City?
You have never seen me here before. Will you

touch me in the same places? Do you come
filled with the same expectations?

IV
FORMS OF LOVE

Night Message

It is hard to believe the stars
are sending light from so many

years ago. That the transmission
of Neptune's likeness took four days

to reach the Earth is unfathomable.
Traveling 186,000 miles per second

is beyond comprehension. No wonder
these nights the sky seems filled

with longing. If there were clouds
we could not see the stars. Then,

who would imagine what the galaxy
is trying to tell us:

We are but a whisper.
A whisper? No, a shooting star—

for the speed of sound is slower
than the speed of light. No wonder

on nights like this the sky
and all watching it are silent.

Forms of Love

1. Instruments of Desire

The surgeon's eyes, gloved hand, the mask
placed over my face. The intravenous drips

into my arm. I breathe deep. The scalpel
tears me open. The first time. Above me

your head rears up, your back, arched,
rises. Your sweat pours into my eyes.

This is how it happens—again and again
when I try to hold your shoulder, the needle

breaks through my arm. And after, when it's
over, I'm left marked by your touch and these

scars. My blood and your ecstasy—
indistinguishable, commingled by time.

2. Illumination

A hot summer night in an open field.
Beneath me, your naked body gives back

the moon. Sweat makes you glisten.
Taking you full in my mouth, your

hands in my hair, my hands holding
your hips, I try to find the answer

in your body. My passion in your eyes.
Your embrace long after you've gone.

I have it memorized—your muscled calves,
your sculpted thighs. I fit your smooth

skin over mine. Now, touching myself
on this hot summer night, I shine.

3. Rapture

Mute. Pinned to the bed. Your body
on top of me again. Your hands hold

my face as our mouths connect. I am
gagged by your tongue. Sounds rise

in my throat and I want to spit you
out of me.

But I bite your lip and the taste of
your blood stifles my cry. Your nails

cut into my wrists and when you break
from me, my blood will stain your palms.

This is how it is—every night, clean,
no words.

4. Night Fire

The smell of burnt flesh. My shadow
climbs the wall. Beside me, your imprint

on my bed. Teeth marks on my skin.
Somewhere in the city you are making

love to another man. Does he writhe
under your touch, like I did? Do you

ride his back? Leave him scarred?
I hear him gasping for air—his face

in his pillow—and I know you won't
let him go until you have finished.

Trapped in his bed, his skin will rise.
Soon, he begins to burn from within.

5. Forms of Love

I am laid out on the table when they come.
Hands mold my body, again and again, until

I am shaped by their desire. Eyes gape
at my distorted form in the hospital bed.

But tonight, your hands move down my thighs.
Your fingers know my scars. Your tongue

surrounds my toes. All they have left I give
to you. My legs around your neck when you

enter me—chest to chest, face to face,
eyes wide open in this full-bodied love.

Shame

On my knees. A motel shower. You face
the wall. My lips trace the back of your

thighs. I let my tongue go where it
wants to go, tamper with the delicate

mysteries—(Why do we do such things?
And in such places?) I part the curtain

of shame—with my tongue—I worship
what cannot be seen. The water pours

over us—scalds our skin as I cleanse
our lives of what we cannot yet name.

Sex Poem

Not in front of the fire, but on
the floor in front of the t.v.—

you position our bodies to see
the video on the screen. The carpet

burns my shoulders. I feel you
enter me. Which body is mine?

There are too many bodies—I want
to tell you to stop—but I mouth

the sounds I hear behind me
as you stroke me into oblivion.

Beauty and Variations

1.

What is it like to be so beautiful? I dip
my hands inside you, come up with—*what?*

Beauty, at birth applied, does not transfer
to my hands. But every night, your hands

touch my scars, raise my twisted limbs to
graze against your lips. Lips that never

form the words—*you are beautiful*—transform
my deformed bones into—*what?*—if not beauty.

Can only one of us be beautiful? Is this your
plan? Are your sculpted thighs more powerful

driving into mine? Your hands find their way
inside me, scrape against my heart. Look

at your hands. Pieces of my skin trail from
your fingers. What do you make of this?

Your hands that know my scars, that lift me to your
lips, now drip my blood. Can blood be beautiful?

2.

I want to break your bones. Make them so
they look like mine. Force you to walk on

twisted legs. Then, will your lips still beg
for mine? Or will that disturb the balance

of our desire? Even as it inspires, your body
terrifies. And once again I find your hands

inside me. Why do you touch my scars? You
can't make them beautiful any more than I can

tear your skin apart. Beneath my scars,
between my twisted bones, hides my heart.

Why don't you let me leave my mark? With no
flaws on your skin—how can I find your heart?

3.

How much beauty can a person bear? Your smooth
skin is no relief from the danger of your eyes.

My hands would leave you scarred. Knead the muscles
of your thighs. I want to tear your skin, reach

inside you—your secrets tightly held. Breathe
deep. Release them. Let them fall into my palms.

My secrets are on my skin. Could this be why
each night I let you deep inside? Is that

where my beauty lies? Your eyes, without secrets,
would be two scars. I want to seal your eyes,

they know my every flaw. Your smooth skin, love's
wounds ignore. My skin won't mend, is callused, raw.

4.

Who can mend my bones? At night, your hands press
into my skin. My feet against your chest, you mold

my twisted bones. What attracts you to my legs? Not
sex. What brings your fingers to my scars is beyond

desire. Why do you persist? Why do you touch me
as if my skin were yours? Seal your lips. No kiss

can heal these wounds. No words unbend my bones.
Beauty is a two-faced god. As your fingers soothe

my scars, they scrape against my heart. Was this
birth's plan—to tie desire to my pain, to stain

love's touch with blood? If my skin won't heal, how
can I escape? My scars are in the shape of my love.

5.

How else can I quench this thirst? My lips
travel down your spine, drink the smoothness

of your skin. I am searching for the core:
What is beautiful? Who decides? Can the laws

of nature be defied? Your body tells me: come
close. But beauty distances even as it draws

me near. What does my body want from yours?
My twisted legs around your neck. You bend

me back. Even though you can't give the bones
at birth I wasn't given, I let you deep inside.

You give me—*what?* Peeling back my skin, you
expose my missing bones. And my heart, long

before you came, just as broken. I don't know who
to blame. So each night, naked on the bed, my body

doesn't want repair, but longs for innocence. If
innocent, despite the flaws I wear, I am beautiful.

The Sacrifice of Desire

If we disengage our lips, I would see your eyes
are closed. Lifting the lids from your eyes, what

will I expose? That night, your body over mine,
our eyes, meeting in a stare, became mirrors:

our bodies' light a glare. Why did you close
your eyes? Why did I blind my own? Our bed

a pyre. Must knowledge always be the sacrifice
of desire? Bend over me again. Don't let that

gentle skin descend over your eyes. This time
keep them open. Release your private fire.

At Risk

After sex, the blood. The cut inside
your lip. The sore on my tongue. Long

after you're gone I will feel you tearing
into me. My body a minefield. I wait

to explode. After sex, I doubt our blood.
But what we did tonight, when we remember,

will be no different. Built on such
mortal moments, love is always a risk

worth taking. After sex, your blood is
my blood. My fate to die in your arms.

NOTES

"Love Poem": "What is it like to be so beautiful?" is from "The Mirror" by Louise Glück in *Descending Figure* (New York: The Ecco Press, 1980).

"Returns": The epigraph, "Don't cut down the trees, I am not yet finished," and "I return to you because you opened me" are quotes by Claude Monet, as they appear in the catalogue for the exhibit *Monet in the '90s: The Series Paintings* by Paul Tucker (New Haven: The Yale University Press, 1990). This poem was written in response to the exhibit and to the catalogue.

"The Healing Notebooks": In (12) lines are quotations, as follows: "There is always something to be made of pain" from "Love Poem" by Louise Glück in *The House on Marshland* (New York: The Ecco Press, 1975); "Ask whose signature is stamped on the orders" from "For the Record" by Adrienne Rich in *Your Native Land, Your Life* (New York: W. W. Norton and Company, 1986); "People with AIDS need drugs not fiction about AIDS" from an interview with Sarah Schulman published in *The Sentinel*, San Francisco, February, 1989; and "Not one of my poems ever saved one Jew" is commonly attributed to W. H. Auden.

"Beauty and Variations": In section 1, "What is it like to be so beautiful?" is from "The Mirror" by Louise Glück, as noted above for "Love Poem." In section 3, "How much beauty can a person bear?" is from "Baskets" by Louise Glück in *The Triumph of Achilles* (New York: The Ecco Press, 1985).

ACKNOWLEDGMENTS

Grateful acknowledgment is made to the editors of the following journals and anthologies in which some of these poems, or earlier versions of them, first appeared and/or were reprinted:

The American Voice: "Beauty and Variations," "Excavation"
Bay Windows: "Brotherly Love"
Confrontation: "Saturn Return," "Surgery"
The Disability Rag: "Body Language," "Incubator," "Excavation," "Learning to Walk," "Transfiguration," "X-Ray"
The Evergreen Chronicles: "Love Poem"
Five Fingers Review: "Anesthesia," "The Healing Notebooks (12)," "The Healing Notebooks (18)," "In These Times"
The James White Review: "Body Language," "Dressing The Wound," "Jerusalem: 1984" (as "In Jerusalem"), "Returns," "The Sacrifice of Desire"
Men's Style: "Solstice"
Mudfish: "Illumination"
OUT/LOOK: "Forms of Love," "Rapture"
The Plum Review: "Night Message"
Provincetown Arts: "At Risk"
Salamander: "To The End"
The Sentinel: "The Burden of Memory"
Slant: "Elegy"

The Western Journal of Medicine: "Body Language," "History," "Incubator," "X-Ray"

"The Healing Notebooks" was published as a chapbook by Open Books, Berkeley, California, 1990, and received the 1991 Gregory Kolovakos Award for AIDS Writing.

"Excavation" and "Love Poem" appeared in *The Disability Studies Reader*, edited by Lennard Davis (Routledge, 1996).

"Love Poem" appeared in *Eros in Boystown* edited by Michael Lassell (Crown, 1996).

"The Healing Notebooks (9)" appeared in *The Name of Love: Classic Gay Love Poems* edited by Michael Lassell (St. Martin's Press, 1995).

"Excavation" appeared in *The Ragged Edge: The Disability Experience from the Pages of the First Fifteen Years of The Disability Rag* edited by Barrett Shaw (Advocado Press, 1994).

"Anesthesia," "Excavation," and "Dressing The Wound" appeared in *Range of Motion*, edited by Cheryl Marie Wade (Squeaky Wheels Press, 1993).

The author thanks the Edward F. Albee Foundation, Blue Mountain Center, Helene Wurlitzer Foundation of New Mexico, Millay Colony for the Arts, Ragdale Foundation, Ucross Foundation, and the Virginia Center for the Creative Arts, for the time, solitude, and inspiration needed to conceive, write, and edit *Anesthesia*. He also thanks the American Academy of Poets, American Academy and Institute for Arts and Letters, Author's League Fund, Carnegie Fund for Writers, Change, Inc., and the PEN Writers' Fund for emergency financial assistance given during the writing of this book.

Many thanks to Colette Inez, Sybil Kollar, Kathryn Levy, Susan Moon, Mary Jane Perna, and Steve Silberman for their editorial suggestions.

ABOUT THE AUTHOR

Kenny Fries received the Gregory Kolvakos Award for AIDS Writing for *The Healing Notebooks*. He is the author of *Body, Remember: A Memoir,* and the editor of *Staring Back: An Anthology of Writers with Disabilites,* both forthcoming from Dutton. His play, *A Human Equation,* premiered at La Mama E.T.C. in New York City. He is the recipient of a grant from the Ludwig Vogelstein Foundation and residencies at The MacDowell Colony and Yaddo. Originally from Brooklyn, New York, he currently lives with the painter Kevin Wolff in Northampton, Massachusetts, and teaches in the MFA in Writing Program at Goddard College.